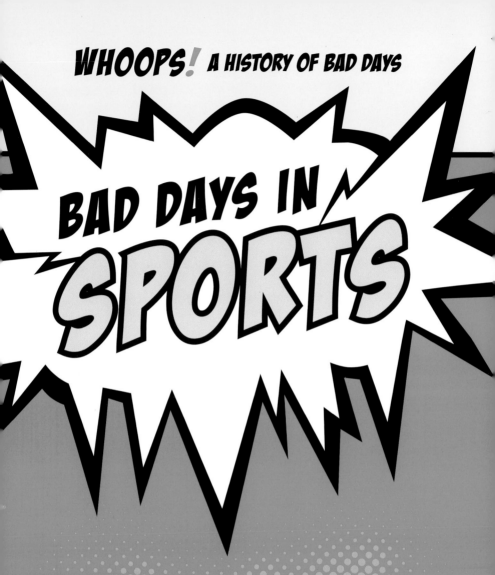

WHOOPS! A HISTORY OF BAD DAYS

BAD DAYS IN SPORTS

BY JON MARTHALER

ignite

CAPSTONE PRESS
a capstone imprint

Ignite is published by Capstone Press, an imprint of Capstone,
1710 Roe Crest Drive, North Mankato, Minnesota 56003
www.mycapstone.com

Library of Congress Cataloging-in-Publication Data
Names: Marthaler, Jon, author.
Title: Bad days in sports / by Jon Marthaler.
Description: North Mankato, Minnesota: An imprint of Capstone Press, [2017]
  | Series: Ignite. Whoops! A History of Bad Days | Includes bibliographical
  references and index. | Audience: Ages: 10-13. | Audience: Grades: 4 to 6.
Identifiers: LCCN 2016031302|
ISBN 9781410985644 (library binding) |
ISBN 9781410985682 (eBook PDF)
Subjects: LCSH: Sports—History—Juvenile literature. |
  Sports—History—Miscellanea—Juvenile literature.
Classification: LCC GV571 .M34 2017 | DDC 796.09—dc23
LC record available at https://lccn.loc.gov/2016031302

Editorial Credits
Melissa York, editor; Nikki Farinella, designer and production specialist

Photo Credits
AP Images, 13, 18, 27, Edward Kitch, 10, *Fort Worth Star-Telegram*, 15, Fred Jewell, 40, NFL
Photos, 36; Getty Images: Bettmann, 11, Jeff J. Mitchell, 29, John Berry, cover, Popperfoto/
Bob Thomas, 20; Icon Sportswire: John McDonough, 25, John Rivera, 12; iStockphoto:
Duncan Walker, 5 (right), flowgraph, 41 (middle left), inktycoon, 22, Patiwit, 41 (top),
willierossin, 19 (field); Jason Bye, 21; Newscom: AFLO Sport/YUTAKA, 33, akg-images, 6,
7, ArtMedia Heritage Images, 4-5, Cal Sport Media/Damon Tarver, 23, Cal Sport Media/
Sportimage/David Klein, 38, EPA/Bagus Indahono, 9, EPA/John G. Mabanglo, 34, EPA/
Justin Lane, 26, MCT/*Chicago Tribune*/Phil Velasquez, 17, MCT/Nhat V. Meyer, 16,
Mirrorpix/Chris Turvey, 14, Photoshot/Talking Sport, 28, Reuters/Brent Smith, 30, Reuters/
Kai Pfaffenbach, 32, Reuters/Mark Baker, 8, Reuters/Mike Stone, 37; Shutterstock, 19
(player icon), 22 (player icon), doodle, 41 (bottom right), Gustavo Fadel, 31, L.E. Mormile,
24, Photo Works, 35, Vasily Smirnov, 39

Design Element: Shutterstock Images: Designer things (bursts, dots, and bubble cloud)

Printed in Canada.
010035S17

TABLE OF CONTENTS

OLD-TIME MESS-UPS

ANCIENT HISTORY

Since the beginning of sports, there have been bad days. You can always count on someone to fall down, forget about the rules, or just lose it. Even when the athletes aren't messing up, the referees can be counted on to get things wrong sometimes.

The first bad day in sports might have happened to the mythological Greek goddess Atalanta, who swore never to get married. Her father, Iasus, demanded that she marry. She agreed, but on one condition. Her potential husband had to beat her in a footrace, or he would be killed. After many young men died trying, Hippomenes sought the help of Aphrodite, the goddess of love, who gave him three golden apples. Using the apples, he tricked Atalanta, defeated her, and wed her. However, Hippomenes wasn't grateful enough to Aphrodite, so the goddess cursed the couple and turned them into lions. Too bad for Atalanta that she didn't win that race!

DID YOU KNOW?

The game of cricket dates back to at least the 1600s. In part, we know this because of a bad day for six people in the English county of Sussex. The six were punished for playing cricket rather than going to church in 1622.

The Greek goddess Atalanta lost her first race when her challenger, Hippomenes, distracted her with golden apples.

Mary, Queen of Scots

OOPS!

Days after her husband was murdered in 1567, Mary, Queen of Scots, decided to head out onto the golf course. Playing a game so soon after her husband's death helped convince her enemies that she was behind the murder. Mary fled to England, where she was locked up and eventually beheaded for political reasons.

THE WORST SPORTS DAY EVER?

The worst day in sports history might have been the day of the 1904 Olympic marathon in Saint Louis, Missouri. The race was run on dusty, unpaved roads. To add to the problems, the temperature that day was more than 90 degrees Fahrenheit (32 degrees Celsius). One man vomited so hard he quit the race. Another was chased off the course by wild dogs. A third inhaled too much dust, collapsed, and nearly died from internal bleeding. The winner, Thomas Hicks, was hallucinating by the end of the race. This was mostly because his support team had been feeding him brandy and raw eggs laced with the poison strychnine because they thought it would help his performance.

FAST FACT

Fred Lorz quit the marathon after 9 miles (14 kilometers) and hitched a ride in a car heading to the finish line. As he got close to the finish, he decided to start running again. After he finished, organizers nearly awarded him the gold medal before he was found out.

Thomas Hicks's day job was professional clown. He retired from marathons permanently after his win.

Thomas Hicks's support team refreshes him at mile 23 (kilometer 37).

HE STILL TOOK FOURTH PLACE!

The person having the worst day, though, was contestant and Cuban mailman Félix Carvajal. He had to walk and hitchhike from New Orleans, Louisiana, to Saint Louis after losing all of his money gambling. He showed up at the starting line in work boots, long wool pants, and a beret. As he ran, he got sick after eating apples he found along the way and had to lay down and take a nap. After all that, he finished fourth and didn't win a medal.

BREAKING ALL THE RULES

IT'S NOT OVER TILL IT'S OVER

At the 2001 Swimming World Championships in Fukuoka, Japan, the Australian women's 4 × 200 freestyle relay team finished first. The three other members of the relay team jumped into the pool to celebrate. Unfortunately for them, the other teams hadn't stopped swimming yet. Because they jumped in the water before the race was finished, the team was disqualified after the race. Great Britain won the race instead.

Giann Rooney of the Australian women's freestyle relay team celebrated too soon.

At the 2010 Winter Olympics in Vancouver, British Columbia, Canada, Sven Kramer finished first in the 10,000-meter speed skating event. After the race, though, he was disqualified. His coach had pointed him to the wrong lane on the track when he was supposed to switch lanes during the race. It cost him a gold medal!

OOPS!

NOT FAR ENOUGH

Australian jockey Rhys McLeod rode Mystic Outlaw in a race at Moonee Valley in Melbourne, Australia, in 2002. The horse galloped for the finish line with 600 meters to go. Whipping his horse all the way, McLeod reached the post 10 lengths ahead. The problem: he'd forgotten that he was riding in a 3,000-meter race. There was still an entire lap of the track to go! After all of the whipping and sprinting, the horse was out of gas. McLeod and Mystic Outlaw finished 72 lengths behind the winner.

Yu Yang (right) and Wang Xiaoli (left) of China play in a competition in Indonesia in 2012, only months before they were banned from the Olympics.

DID YOU KNOW?

Four badminton teams at the 2012 Olympics in London—two South Korean, one Indonesian, and one Chinese—tried to lose matches to improve their chances in the knockout round. They tried things such as serving the shuttlecock directly into the net or directly out of bounds. Officials banned all four teams for trying to lose.

Caddies aren't allowed to ride in carts during tournaments—even when nature calls. Lisa McCloskey was given a two-shot penalty at the 2010 U.S. Women's Open because her caddie took a golf cart to go to the bathroom.

OOPS!

BIG MISTAKE!

Argentinian golfer Roberto De Vicenzo finished in a tie for the championship of the Masters in Augusta, Georgia, in 1968. Course officials started to prepare for a playoff. Then they noticed that De Vicenzo had signed a scorecard with a mistake. According to his scorecard, De Vicenzo had shot a 66, not the 65 he actually shot. This meant he lost to American Bob Goalby by one stroke. Exclaimed De Vicenzo, "I lose my brain. ... Now all I can think of is what a stupid [man] I am."

Roberto de Vincenzo had a hall-of-fame career but never won the Masters.

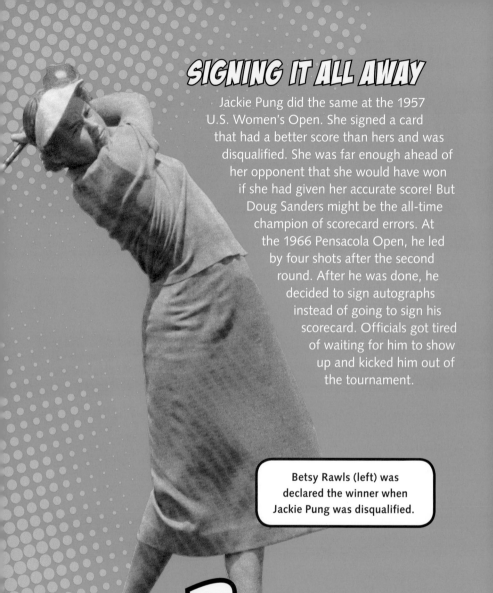

SIGNING IT ALL AWAY

Jackie Pung did the same at the 1957 U.S. Women's Open. She signed a card that had a better score than hers and was disqualified. She was far enough ahead of her opponent that she would have won if she had given her accurate score! But Doug Sanders might be the all-time champion of scorecard errors. At the 1966 Pensacola Open, he led by four shots after the second round. After he was done, he decided to sign autographs instead of going to sign his scorecard. Officials got tired of waiting for him to show up and kicked him out of the tournament.

> Betsy Rawls (left) was declared the winner when Jackie Pung was disqualified.

DID YOU KNOW?

Even the simplest training devices are banned during golf tournaments. Juli Inkster found this out during a 2010 tournament in Portland, Oregon. Inkster swung her club with a weighted donut attached to loosen up during her round. After the round, she was disqualified.

WHAT WERE THEY THINKING?

TOO MUCH TIME

University of Connecticut basketball player Roscoe Smith took a shot at glory in 2011. UConn and Texas were tied late in a January 8 game. Smith grabbed a missed shot and heaved it to the other end of the court to try to beat the buzzer. Unfortunately for Smith, there were still 11 seconds on the clock. His team had plenty of time to try something other than a 75-foot (23-meter) heave. Luckily for Smith, Texas missed their shot too, and UConn held on to win. Amazingly, the next year he did the same thing at the end of the first half of another game. This time, though, there were only four seconds left.

Roscoe Smith went on to play professional basketball for a team in Greece.

Rosie Ruiz falsely claimed the laurel crown of victory.

FAST FACT

Rosie Ruiz crossed the finish line as the women's winner of the Boston Marathon in near-world-record time in 1980. Fans said she looked like she had hardly sweated. Days later, they found out why: she had sneaked onto the course 1 mile (1.6 km) from the finish line and run only the last small portion of the race.

NEVER MIND!

South African Thomas Hamilton-Brown thought he'd lost his first lightweight boxing match at the 1936 Olympics in Berlin, Germany. To cheer himself up, he went on an eating binge. Later that day, a scoring error was found. Hamilton-Brown had won the fight after all and was still in contention for a medal. Unfortunately, he was disqualified the next day when, due to his eating, he was found to be five pounds (2.3 kilograms) overweight.

DID YOU KNOW?

During a speech in 2015, U.K. Prime Minister David Cameron briefly forgot which was his favorite soccer team. "I'd rather you supported West Ham," he said, forgetting that he'd previously told reporters that Aston Villa was his favorite.

EPIC MELTDOWN

Golfer Jean van de Velde came to the final hole of the 1999 Open Championship at Carnoustie Golf Links in Scotland with a three-shot lead. He knew that all he needed to do was make the par-four hole in six strokes, a double bogey, and he'd win the title. Instead of playing safe, though, he decided to hit a driver. His drive landed over on the next hole. His second shot hit the grandstand. His third shot went in the water. After a penalty stroke, his fifth shot went in the bunker. He managed to make a seven on the hole to get into a playoff—which he lost.

Jean van de Velde tries to keep his sense of humor as he plays from the water after his third shot.

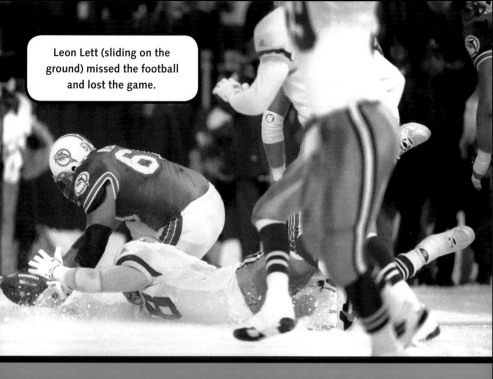

Leon Lett (sliding on the ground) missed the football and lost the game.

DON'T TOUCH THE BALL!

In a November 1993 football game, the Dallas Cowboys blocked a last-minute Miami Dolphins field goal. All the Cowboys had to do to win was not touch the ball. For some reason, Dallas defensive tackle Leon Lett tried to fall on the ball. Instead, it bounced off his shin, and Miami recovered it. That gave the Dolphins another field goal try with three seconds left. They made it, and in part because of Lett's blunder, the Cowboys lost.

Near the end of the National Collegiate Athletic Association (NCAA) Championship basketball game between Michigan and North Carolina in 1993, Michigan trailed by two points. Michigan forward Chris Webber grabbed a rebound and called a timeout his team didn't have. North Carolina got two free throws and the ball. Then another Michigan foul put North Carolina up 77–71, ending any chance of a Michigan comeback.

OOPS!

(DON'T) TAKE A TIMEOUT

At the 2012 Olympics in London, the U.S. women's water polo team led Australia by a single goal. There was just one second left to play. All the United States had to do was let the one second run off the clock. Instead the American coach tried to call timeout while Australia had the ball. In water polo, that means the other team gets a penalty shot. Australia made the shot and tied the score to send the game into overtime. Fortunately for the U.S. team, they won in overtime.

U.S. player Maggie Steffens tries to pass past an Australian player during the teams' Olympics matchup.

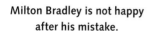

Milton Bradley is not happy after his mistake.

In a 2009 baseball game, Chicago Cubs right fielder Milton Bradley caught a high flying ball. He tossed it to a lucky fan in the crowd to celebrate the third out. The problem? There were only two outs, so the inning was not over. Two runners got an extra base as a result.

OOPS!

KEEP YOUR PANTS ON!

After sliding into first base in 1990, Chicago White Sox baseball player Steve Lyons felt a little dirt in his shorts. He unbuckled his pants and dropped them to his knees to dust himself off. But he forgot that he was still standing on first base! Luckily for Lyons, he had knee-length shorts underneath his uniform pants. His shorts prevented an even more embarrassing day.

NO, THE OTHER WAY

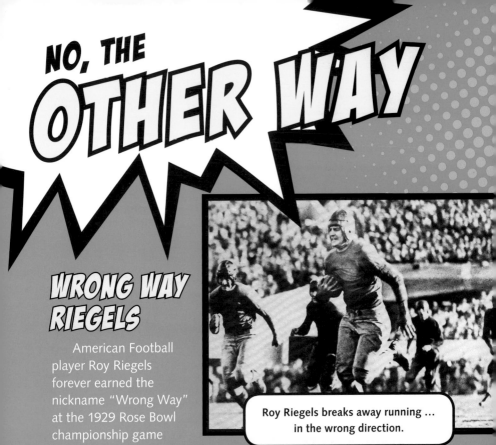

Roy Riegels breaks away running …
in the wrong direction.

WRONG WAY RIEGELS

American Football player Roy Riegels forever earned the nickname "Wrong Way" at the 1929 Rose Bowl championship game in California. Playing linebacker for the University of California, Berkeley, Riegels picked up a Georgia Tech fumble and ran 60 yards—but toward his own end zone. His teammates managed to tackle him on the one-yard line. Cal tried to punt on the next play, but Georgia Tech blocked the kick for a safety. Georgia Tech won 8–7, thanks in part to Riegels' run.

HALFWAY TO HAWAII

Jim Marshall did Riegels one better in 1964. Playing for the Minnesota Vikings, he picked up a fumble by San Francisco and dashed 66 yards. Unlike Riegels, though, he actually made it to the end zone. He then threw the ball to his teammates on the sideline. Officials ruled the play a safety, giving two points to San Francisco, but the Vikings won anyway. After the game, Marshall's teammates asked him to fly the plane home from San Francisco. They joked that he'd land them in Hawaii! A few weeks after the game, he received a note from Riegels: "Welcome to the club."

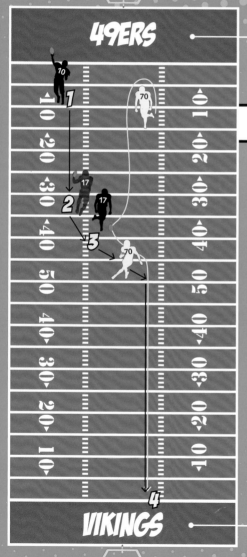

49ERS

END ZONE

Jim Marshall's Wrong Way Run

1 San Francisco 49ers quarterback Georgia Mira (10) tossed a pass downfield to running back Billy Kilmer (17).

2 Kilmer caught the pass and tried to run, but he was hit and fumbled.

3 Minnesota Vikings defensive end Jim Marshall (70) picked up the fumble but was turned the wrong way.

4 Marshall sprinted into the wrong end zone, then threw the ball out of bounds in celebration. The play was ruled a safety.

VIKINGS

END ZONE

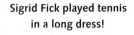

Sigrid Fick played tennis in a long dress!

At the 1912 Summer Olympics in Stockholm, Sweden, tennis partners Gunnar Setterwall and Sigrid Fick of Sweden were playing for the mixed doubles gold medal. Unfortunately, Fick got a bit mixed up. She hit Setterwall in the face with her racket. Understandably, the two struggled after that, and they lost the gold medal match.

OOPS!

NOT-SO-FREE THROW

Women's basketball superstar Lauren Jackson once burned her team by grabbing a rebound and putting the ball in the hoop—the wrong hoop. Jackson, playing for the Seattle Storm, got turned around during a 2002 game against the Los Angeles Sparks. The Sparks missed a free throw, and Jackson hauled in the rebound and scored in the wrong basket. It helped Los Angeles pull away, and the Storm lost 80–68—thanks in part to Jackson.

DID YOU KNOW?

Baseball player Tommy John, pitching for the New York Yankees in 1988, made three errors on the same play. He fumbled a ball that was bunted to him (error #1). He threw the ball away trying to catch the runner at first base (#2). Then he cut off a throw going toward home plate and threw wildly again (#3).

THE WRONG BIKE?

Belgian cyclist Femke van den Driessche took the wrong way to a whole new level at the 2016 cyclocross world championships in Heusden-Zolder, Belgium. Van den Driessche, then 19 years old, was one of the favorites in the women's under-23 race. She was forced to drop out due to "mechanical problems." This was a nice way of saying that she had an electric motor concealed in the frame of her bike! She tried to claim that it was a friend's bike that she mistakenly used for the race. Officials didn't buy her story and suspended her for six years. They also made her return all of her medals.

Femke van den Driessche was the first person found guilty of "mechanical doping," or enhancing her performance with a machine, in the sport of cycling.

A soccer game between Grimsby Town and Hartlepool United in 2016 was delayed. Grimsby Town's team drove to the wrong stadium, 30 minutes away. It seemed to have an effect on them. Grimsby lost 2–1.

THAT WASN'T THE GOAL!

The nerves of the 1986 hockey playoffs got to the Edmonton Oilers' Steve Smith. In Game 7 of a series, he accidentally scored a goal into his own net. Standing behind his net, Smith tried to pass the puck to a teammate. The puck hit his goalie and rebounded into the net. The goal gave the Calgary Flames a 3–2 lead. Calgary held on for the win, ending Edmonton's season.

Steve Smith's Own Goal

1 The Calgary Flames shoot the puck into the Edmonton Oilers zone.

2 Edmonton's Steve Smith (5) gathers the puck behind the Oilers net.

3 Smith tries to pass the puck to a teammate, but it hits goaltender Grant Fuhr (31) and rebounds into the net.

WARDROBE MALFUNCTION

Arizona Coyotes goalie Mike Smith scored one of the strangest goals ever—with his pants. During a 2013 overtime game against the Buffalo Sabres, the puck was batted into the air. Smith lost sight of it. He scrambled back into his own net to try to keep the puck out. But the airborne puck had landed on his back and slid down into his pants. When he got into the net, still looking for the puck, the referees ruled the puck had crossed the goal line. The goal gave Buffalo the win in overtime.

In the 1985 National Football Conference (NFC) Championship Game, Sean Landeta was the punter for the New York Giants. He tried to punt from his own end zone—and missed his kick. The Chicago Bears recovered the fumble and scored a touchdown. It was a long day for Landeta and the Giants, who lost 21–0.

OOPS!

ON THE CLOCK

IF YOU SNOOZE, YOU LOSE

American golfer Jim Furyk had a 7:30 a.m. tee time for a 2010 tournament in Paramus, New Jersey. He set the alarm clock on his cell phone. Unfortunately, his phone died overnight. He woke up with just seven minutes to make it to the course. Panicked, he showed up at the course late, with his shoes untied and no belt or socks. Officials promptly disqualified him.

Despite his tournament troubles, Jim Furyk was named the PGA Tour Player of the Year in 2010.

Runner Siegfried "Wim" Esejas was set to be Suriname's first-ever competitor at the Olympic Games in Rome in 1960. Unfortunately, he was given the wrong time for his heat in the 800 meters. He slept soundly through his chance at Olympic glory.

OOPS!

SLEEPING IT ALL AWAY

British triathlete Jody George could have done without a snooze button. George spent a year raising money for charity for his participation in the Weymouth triathlon in 2014. On the day of the race, his alarm went off at 3:00 a.m. But George hit snooze—and next woke up at 5:55 a.m. It was far too late for him to make it to the race. He later made up for his blunder by running his own version of the triathlon.

Dennis Rodman played for the San Antonio Spurs from 1993 to 1995, but he was more famously known as a member of the Chicago Bulls from 1995 to 1998.

DID YOU KNOW?

Basketball player Dennis Rodman, then with the San Antonio Spurs, slept right through the start of a game in 1995. Rodman showed up 35 minutes after the game started, but amazingly, his team did not suspend him.

TRYING TIMES

Ramon Castro, catcher for the New York Mets baseball team, was scheduled to start in San Diego, California, in 2008. But he was pulled from the lineup after showing up late. Castro's excuse was that his pocket schedule said the game was at 4:00 p.m., not 1:00 p.m. His schedule was right, but only in the eastern time zone. San Diego is in the Pacific time zone, three hours earlier. The game went ahead—without Castro—at 1:00.

FAST FACT

Iranian boxer Ali Kazemi missed his bus to the arena for his event at the 1992 Summer Olympics in Barcelona, Spain. He had to take a taxi in a hurry. He made it in time, but he showed up for his match without headgear or boxing gloves. He was not ready to fight and was disqualified.

Ramon Castro played his last professional game in 2011.

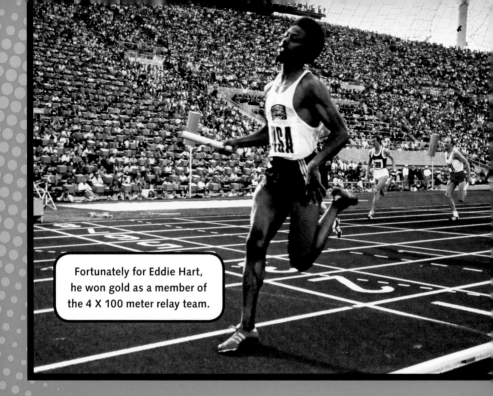

Fortunately for Eddie Hart, he won gold as a member of the 4 X 100 meter relay team.

TV TIMEOUT

At the 1972 Summer Olympics in Munich, Germany, U.S. sprinters Eddie Hart and Rey Robinson raced in the morning. The two both qualified for the 100-meter quarterfinals. At 4:00 p.m., they dropped by the ABC television building. There, they saw the quarterfinal heats taking place live on TV—an hour and a half before they expected. Someone had given them the wrong start time! They both rushed to the track, but they arrived too late to run. They had both been favored to medal in the race. Neither even had a chance.

OOPS!

During spring training in 2006, Chicago Cubs pitcher Edwin Jackson used his phone's GPS to direct him to the Oakland A's baseball stadium. Upon arriving at Phoenix Municipal Stadium, he found the area deserted. He found out the A's had moved to another park at the end of the previous year.

TAKING THE
FALL

SPECTACULAR FALL

Devon Loch was one of the favorites in the 1956 Grand National horse race in England. The mother of England's Queen Elizabeth II owned the horse. Dick Francis was the jockey. Francis was looking good to claim some royal glory, as the horse had a huge lead. Without warning, as the horse raced down the stretch, it jumped in the air and slid along the ground—losing the race. No one could figure out why Devon Loch jumped.

People speculate Devon Loch jumped because he had a cramp, because he saw a shadow, or because the crowd noise startled him—but no one knows.

Bulgarian hurdler Vania Stambolova had a very short outing in the 2012 Olympics in London. In her first heat of the 400-meter hurdles, she tripped over the first barrier. Knowing she couldn't win, she walked off the track after just one hurdle.

The press had fun with Vania's last name after her fall because it sounds similar to "stumble over."

NOT HER GOAL

Japanese soccer goalkeeper Ayumi Kaihori wasn't having a good day in the 2015 Women's World Cup Final in Vancouver, British Columbia, Canada. In the first 15 minutes of the game, the United States had already scored three goals. When U.S. midfielder Carli Lloyd stole the ball at the halfway line, though, things got worse for Kaihori. Lloyd launched a shot from midfield. Kaihori tried to backpedal to catch it, but she stumbled and fell down. The ball went off the goalkeeper's fingers, off the post, and into the net.

BAD TIME TO CRASH

At the 2011 Indy 500 car race, rookie J. R. Hildebrand had a comfortable lead on the final lap. At the fourth and final turn, though, he moved to avoid another car. He lost control, smashing into the wall. Dan Wheldon won the race instead. Wheldon finished just ahead of Hildebrand, whose broken car slid across the finish line in second place.

J. R. Hildebrand's crash left his car bent out of shape.

FAST FACT

At the 1993 IndyCar Phoenix Grand Prix car race, Paul Tracy had lapped everyone in the field—twice. With about 30 laps to go, though, his team told him to be careful. Distracted, he spun out and crashed!

Jean Alesi's otherwise successful career spanned more than 20 years.

Jean Alesi ignored his team lap after lap at the 1997 Australian Grand Prix in Melbourne as they screamed at him on the radio that he needed to refuel. Not surprisingly, he ran out of gas while he was in the lead and couldn't finish the race.

OOPS!

JUST GO HOME

Ayrton Senna dominated the 1988 Monaco Grand Prix. This began in the qualifying race, when Senna finished nearly a second and a half faster than teammate Alain Prost. He was also nearly three seconds faster than anyone else. On race day, Senna had gone so far ahead—nearly 50 seconds—that the cameras stopped following him. The next time anyone saw him, he was climbing out of his crashed car. He had lost his concentration and spun into a barrier. He was so upset he didn't even go back to the pit lane. He simply walked off the course and went home to his Monaco apartment.

NO, DON'T GET UP

A steeplechase running race involves plenty of water. Runners hurdle over barriers and splash through pools. At the 3,000-meter race at the 2015 Women's World Championships in Beijing, China, Panama's Rolanda Bell found a different way to get through the water—face-first. Bell misjudged her jump over the barrier. Instead of going over and continuing the race, she took a headfirst dive into the watery pit. Not surprisingly, she finished last in her heat. She did not qualify for the final.

Rolanda Bell went head first into the water.

Hubertus von Hohenlohe was in good spirits despite his Olympic slip-up.

A PRINCELY FALL

Skier Prince Hubertus von Hohenlohe competed in the slalom at the 2014 Winter Olympics in Sochi at the age of 55. Though he is a German prince, he was born in Mexico City. This made him eligible to ski for Mexico, a country that only rarely has snow. The prince wore a ski suit that made him look as if he was in a Mexican mariachi band. In the race, the prince was far behind a gold-medal pace and then crashed halfway down the hill. Still, just competing in the Olympics is pretty good for a senior citizen!

Cyclist Lizzie Armitstead crossed the line in the first stage of the 2015 Women's Tour in England in first place but ran into trouble afterward. Armitstead took her hands off her bike to celebrate. She then crashed into a row of photographers. She missed the remainder of the race due to injury.

OOPS!

NO ONE LIKES A SHOW-OFF

CELEBRATING EARLY

At the 2006 Winter Olympics in Turin, Italy, American Lindsey Jacobellis was leading by a huge margin in the snowboard cross medal race. As she went over the second-to-last jump, she decided to show off a bit. She grabbed her board for a flourish to make the win more exciting. The move unbalanced her, though, and she fell. It cost her the gold medal, which went to Tanja Frieden of Switzerland, who passed her.

Lindsey Jacobellis grabs her board seconds before the resulting tumble causes her to lose first place.

At the 1991 Canadian Grand Prix car race, Nigel Mansell was winning by such a distance that he slowed down to wave at his fans. Then his car died. He slowed to a stop and lost the race to Nelson Piquet. No one is sure if Mansell hit a switch while waving.

OOPS!

TO COOL TO PLAY

In a 2011 summer tournament match, soccer player Mario Balotelli of Manchester City decided to get fancy. After beating the final defender, he twirled around and attempted a show-off back-heeled shot. It wasn't even close, flying 10 feet (3 m) wide of the goal. Adding insult to injury, his coach, Roberto Mancini, immediately removed him from the game, even though it was only midway through the first half. Mancini didn't like Balotelli's show-off attitude.

Mario Balotelli would soon be benched in the 2011 game against the L.A. Galaxy in California.

DID YOU KNOW?

Runner Adriana Pirtea thought she had won the 2007 Chicago Marathon. She waved to fans at the finish line—and didn't see Berhane Adere sprinting to catch her until there were only 55 yards (50 m) to go. Adere won, and Pirtea finished second.

GRIDIRON SHOW-OFF

In Super Bowl XXVII in 1993, Dallas Cowboys defensive tackle Leon Lett picked up a fumble and ran 65 yards to the end zone. As he approached the goal line, though, he slowed down and held the ball out to showboat. Buffalo Bills wide receiver Don Beebe caught him from behind and knocked the ball out of his hand before he scored. Lett's Cowboys still won 52–17. But Lett missed his chance to score in a Super Bowl.

Leon Lett was upset after his fumble.

DID YOU KNOW?

Bill Gramatica, a kicker for the Arizona Cardinals, paid for his celebration right away. Gramatica leapt into the air to celebrate making a field goal in 2001. He landed awkwardly and tore a ligament in his knee.

Cleveland Browns linebacker Dwayne Rudd thought he'd sacked the Kansas City Chiefs' quarterback to end a 2002 game. Instead, the play was still in progress. Rudd was called for a penalty for celebrating. The Chiefs were allowed to run another play. They kicked a field goal, and the Browns lost.

OOPS!

MR. FUMBLES

Wide receiver DeSean Jackson made a career of accidentally failing to score. In 2008, while playing for the Philadelphia Eagles, he caught a long pass behind the Dallas Cowboys defense. As he ran into the end zone for a touchdown, though, he dropped the ball on the one-yard line—a fumble, not a touchdown. It was a trend for him. During 2005, when playing in a high school all-star game, he attempted to cartwheel into the end zone on a long pass. When his hand hit the ground, he lost the ball. Instead of an easy touchdown, it was a fumble.

DeSean Jackson catches the ball he is about to drop on the one-yard line.

THE WRONG CALL

REFEREE BLUNDERS

Soccer referees don't go on the field with much equipment, but what little they have is quite necessary. Premier League soccer official Peter Walton found that out to his cost in 2011. He went to caution Birmingham City's Jordon Mutch in the first half. When he reached in his pocket, he found out he'd forgotten his yellow card. With no other option, he faked flashing the card at Mutch. The penalty stuck, but it went down in history with a laugh as the dreaded "invisible card."

Peter Walton remembered his red card for the Chelsea versus Everton match on January 8, 2008.

OOPS!

In an elimination final in Australia's National Rugby League in 2013, Cronulla beat North Queensland. Later, though, replay showed they'd scored a try on an extra seventh tackle. Referee Matt Cecchin lost track of the count, calling out "four" after the fifth tackle. Somehow the other five match officials lost count at the same time.

STOP AND COUNT TO THREE

At the 2006 World Cup in Germany, English referee Graham Poll took charge of a group soccer game between Croatia and Australia. He gave Croatian left back Josip Simunic a yellow card in the first half and then another in the second. That should have resulted in a red card and Simunic leaving the game. Instead, Poll forgot he'd already carded Simunic, who was allowed to play on. Simunic then earned another yellow card, his third! Poll finally sent Simunic off but was ridiculed for losing track of his cautions. He retired from international refereeing after the error.

Svetlana Khorkina shows her usual balance and poise on the balance beam.

DID YOU KNOW?

During the women's gymnastics event at the 2000 Summer Olympics in Sydney, Australia, half the gymnasts in the competition did their vaults. Then officials discovered that the vault had been set 2 inches (5 centimeters) too low. This had thrown some of the competitors off. The vault was reset and the gymnasts got to do it over. But the pressure got to favorite Svetlana Khorkina of Russia. She failed to medal and blamed the redo.

ORGANIZATIONAL NIGHTMARES

The Chicago White Sox needed to attract more fans to a baseball game in 1979. They came up with the idea of holding Disco Demolition Night. Fans could bring their disco records to be blown up between the two games of a doubleheader. Consumed by their dislike of disco music, the fans stormed the field and ripped up the bases. Some fans tried to climb into the owner's box. The second game had to be canceled.

The police had to break up the riot on the White Sox's field.

UNEXPECTED DROP-INS

The University of North Carolina arranged for two people to parachute into the stadium before a football game in 2008 and present the officials with the game ball. Unfortunately, the duo parachuted into the stadium at Duke University, 8 miles (13 km) away, surprising officials who were waiting for their own game to start.

North Korea flag

At the 2012 Olympics in London, organizers were forced to apologize to North Korea. The North Korea women's soccer team was introduced with South Korean flags accompanying the players' photos on the scoreboard. The game was delayed for an hour while North Korean players refused to come out of their locker room.

OOPS!

South Korea flag

"Jacques Plante" on the Stanley Cup

DID YOU KNOW?

The National Hockey League engraves the names of winning players on the Stanley Cup, its championship trophy. Over the years, there have been several spelling errors. Montreal Canadiens goaltender Jacques Plante won the trophy five years in a row. His name is spelled a different way each year.

J. PLANTE

JACQUES PLANTE

JAC PLANTE

JACQ PLANTE

JAQUES PLANTE

FUN FACTS

*G*olf has many goofy rules. For example, the U.S. and U.K. rules state what happens if a player's golf ball lands near a cactus. The player can wrap himself or herself in a towel to protect against being stuck. However, putting a towel over the cactus is a penalty.

*T*he Formula One Monaco Grand Prix is unique in that part of the racetrack runs next to the Monaco harbor. Two drivers—Alberto Ascari in 1955 and Paul Hawkins in 1965—have accidentally flipped their cars into the harbor during a race!

*A*t the 2004 Olympics in Athens, Greece, Brazilian marathon runner Vanderlei de Lima was leading all the other runners by 38 seconds. With just 5 miles (8 km) to go, a crazed fan ran onto the course and tackled him. This cut into de Lima's lead. He slowed down and was passed by two other runners. He did recover to win the bronze medal.

*T*he sport of shooting has always been a part of the Summer Olympics. The organizers of the 1900 Summer Olympics in Paris, France, though, took it to new heights. For the first and only time, competitors shot at live pigeons.

The world's weirdest sport might be cheese rolling. Competitors at Cooper's Hill in Gloucester, United Kingdom, chase a large wheel of cheese down a very steep hill. It's very dangerous. The final race was delayed in 2005 because the ambulance service had to clear all of the injured people from previous races off the course.

There are 11 ways to get out in cricket, but some happen less often than others. For example, Len Hutton of England is the only person in Test cricket history to be out for obstructing the field. In 1951 he hit the ball straight up into the air, then knocked it away on the way down as the wicketkeeper tried to catch it.

In the history of the Rugby World Cup, only 17 players have been given a red card and sent off from the game. Three of those 17 happened at the same time in one match. In the 1995 World Cup in South Africa, the South African and Canadian teams got into a brawl during their match. Three players were sent off, but replays showed that many more players probably should have been sent off as well.

There are no left-handed sticks in field hockey. Players can only use one side of the stick. Pity the poor lefties who wish to play!

GLOSSARY

back-heel (BAK-heel)—(soccer) move in which the ball is contacted with the back of the heel to pass or shoot

bunt (BUHNT)—(baseball) intentionally short, soft hit by a baseball hitter; used to gain a tactical advantage

caution (KAW-shuhn)—(soccer) yellow card

cyclocross (SYE-klo-kraws)—form of bicycle racing in which the course usually includes both off-road and on-road trails

field goal (FEELD GOHL)—(American football) a play in which a football is kicked through the goalposts for three points

gridiron (GRID-eye-urn)—the field of play in American football, sometimes called gridiron football

interception (in-tur-CEPT-shuhn)—(American football) a pass caught by a player on defense

length (LENGKTH)—(horse racing) measure of distance between horses in a race; one length is one horse from nose to tail

par-four (PAHR-for)—(golf) hole on which it is generally accepted that it will take four shots to get the ball in the hole; golf scores are reported as related to par

sack (SAK)—(American football) tackling the quarterback to the ground while he has the football

safety (SAYF-tee)—(American football) when a player with the football is tackled in his own end zone; the defensive team is awarded two points and the ball

shuttlecock (SHUHT-uhl-kahk)—(badminton) ball used for badminton matches; it has a small, rounded base and feathers attached to slow the shuttlecock, or "birdie"

steeplechase (STEE-puhl-chase)—(track and field) track race that involves barriers and water jumps

strychnine (STRIKE-nine)—a poison; people once thought that the convulsions it caused were good for you (they aren't)

Test cricket (TEST KRIK-it)—longest, five-day-long form of cricket

touchdown (TUHCH-doun)—(American football) a six-point score made by moving the ball over an opposing team's goal line

FIND OUT MORE

BOOKS

Birmingham, Maria. *Weird Zone: Sports.* Toronto: Owlkids Books, 2013.

Chandler, Matt. *Wacky Baseball Trivia: Fun Facts for Every Fan.* North Mankato, Minn.: Capstone, 2016.

Editors of Sports Illustrated Kids. *What Are the Chances? The Wildest Plays in Sports.* New York: Time Home Entertainment, 2014.

Hawkins, Jeff. *Biggest Chokes in Sports.* Minneapolis: Abdo, 2014.

National Geographic Kids. *Weird but True! Sports.* Washington, D.C.: National Geographic, 2016.

PLACES TO VISIT

National Baseball Hall of Fame and Museum
25 Main Street
Cooperstown, NY 13326
http://baseballhall.org/
The National Baseball Hall of Fame and Museum pays tribute to the legends of the sport.

Sports Museum of Los Angeles
1900 S. Main Street
Los Angeles, CA 90007
http://www.sportsmuseumla.com/
The Sports Museum of Los Angeles features exhibits and memorabilia focusing on baseball history and Los Angeles sports teams.

FURTHER RESEARCH

Try to find the worst day in your favorite sport. You can find videos of infamously bad days on youtube.com, search the Internet for epic blunders in almost any sport, or visit the website of your favorite league and search for some of the worst days anyone's ever had.

Find out more about your favorite athlete. Look for books in the library or visit his or her official website for biographies and stats. Has your favorite athlete ever made a blooper reel?

WEBSITES

FactHound offers a safe, fun way to find Internet sites related to this book. All of the sites on FactHound have been researched by our staff.

Here's all you do:

Visit *www.facthound.com*

Type in this code: 9781410985644

Check out projects, games and lots more at
www.capstonekids.com

INDEX